I Can Draw and Trace Dog Faces

AF481943

Husky
Shih Tzu
3
4
6
7
9
10
12
13
Boxer
Jack Russell
St. Bernard
15
16
18
19
21
22
24
25
Chihuahua
Schnauzer
Great Dane
27
28
30
31
33
34
36
37
German shepherd
Bulldog
Golden Retriever
English Bulldog
39
40
42
43
45
46
48
49
Poodle
Dalmatian
Dachshund
51
52
54
55
57
58
Dog food
Dog collar
Dog bone
60
61
63
64
66
67

Husky

1

2

3

4

5

6

7

8

9

Shih Tzu

1 2 3 4

5 6 7 8

9 10 11 12

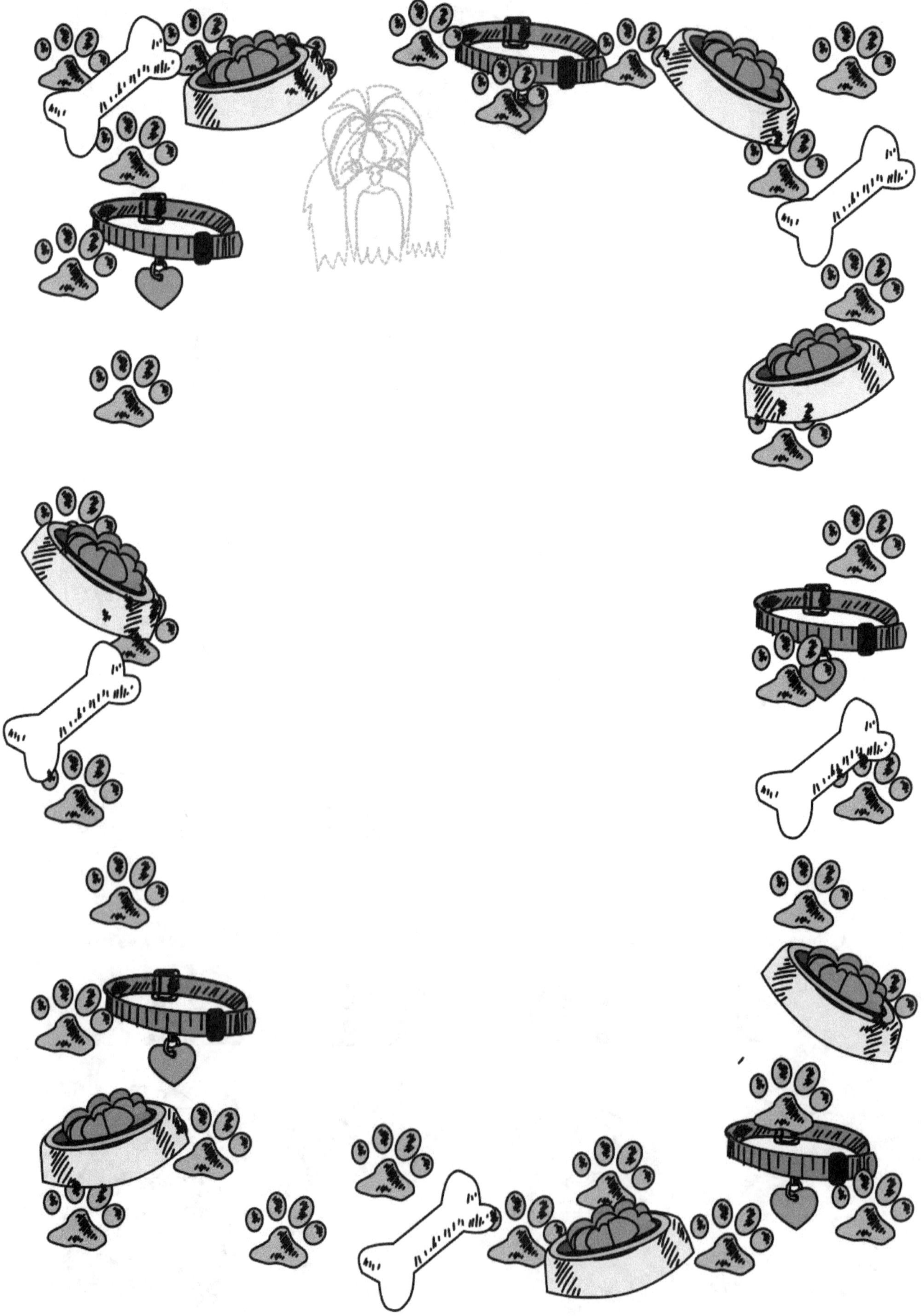

1

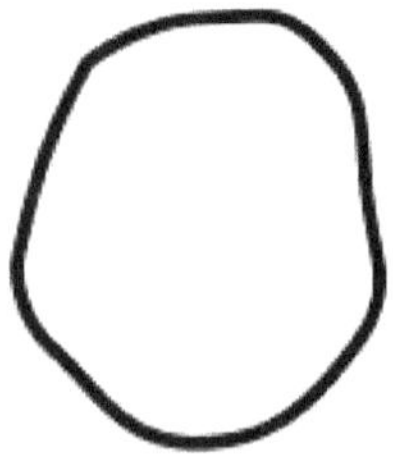

2

3

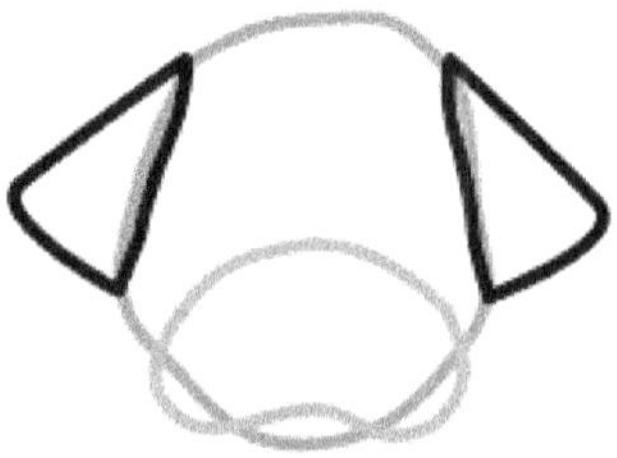

4

5

6

7

8

9

10

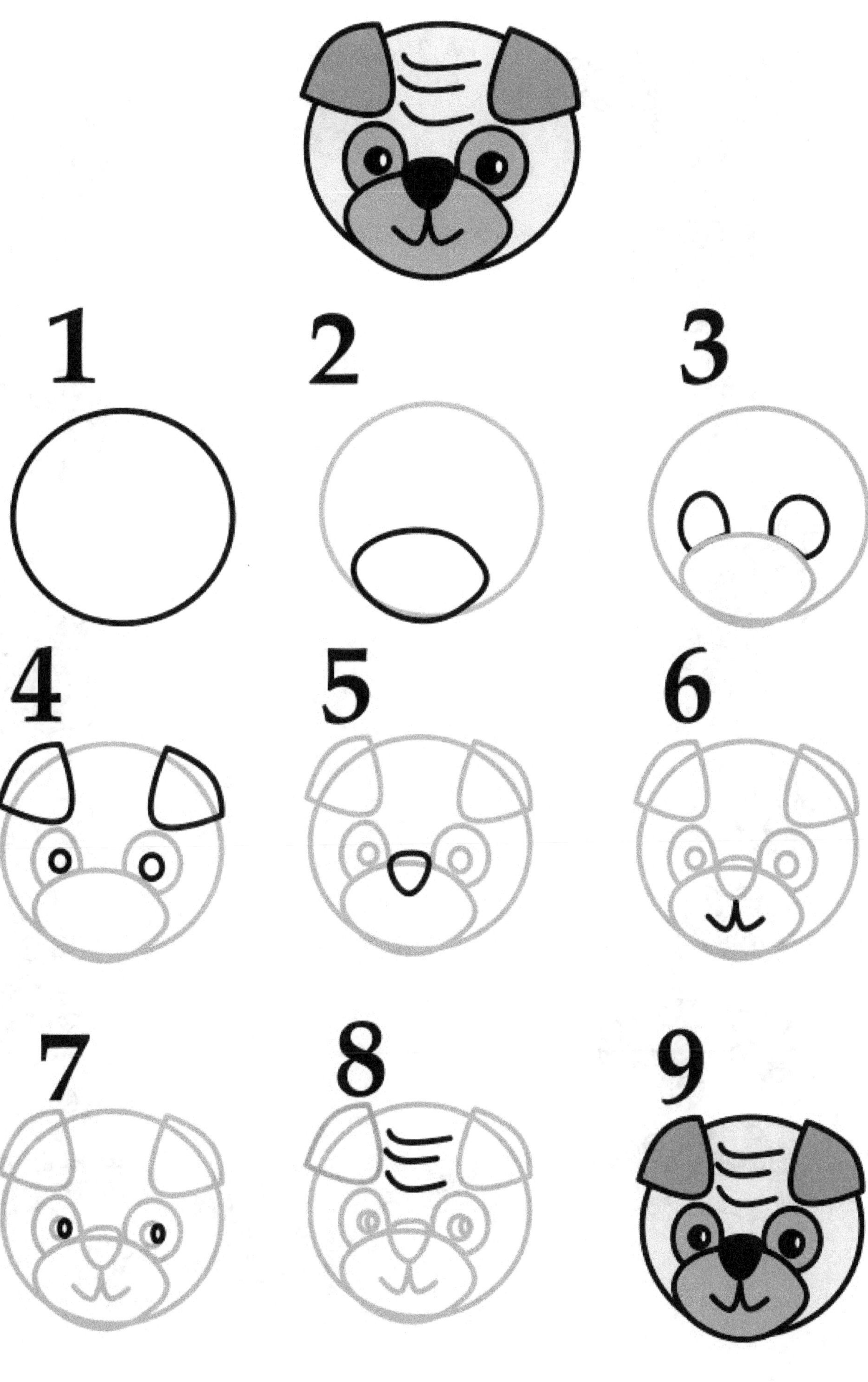

1
2
3
4
5
6
7
8
9

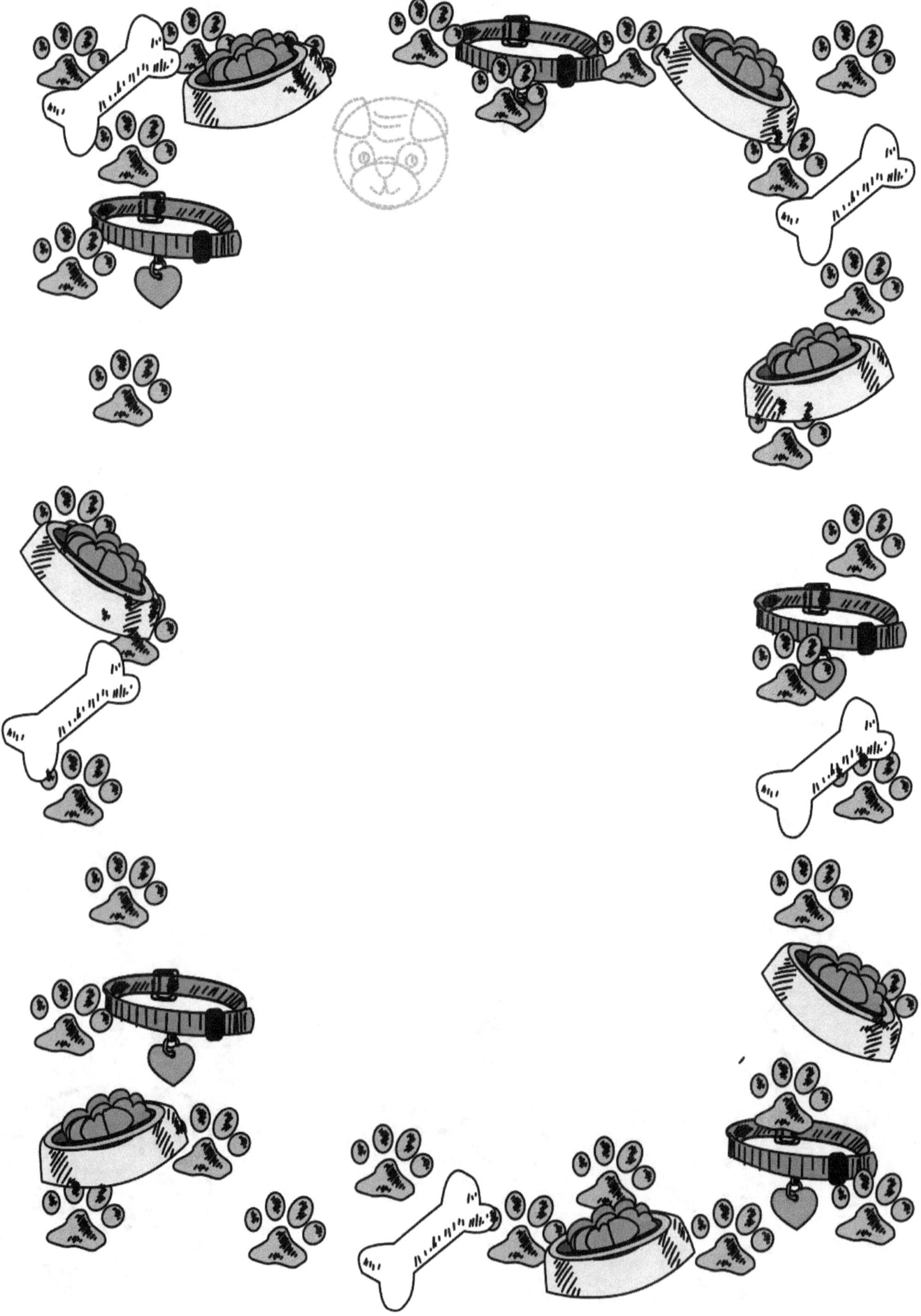

Boxer

1

2

3

4

5

6
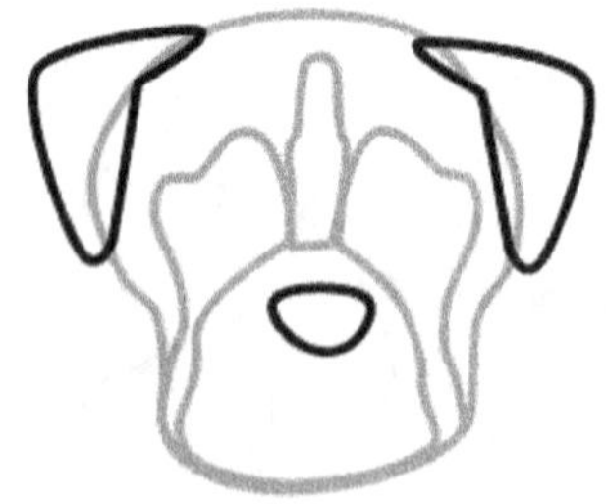

7

8

9

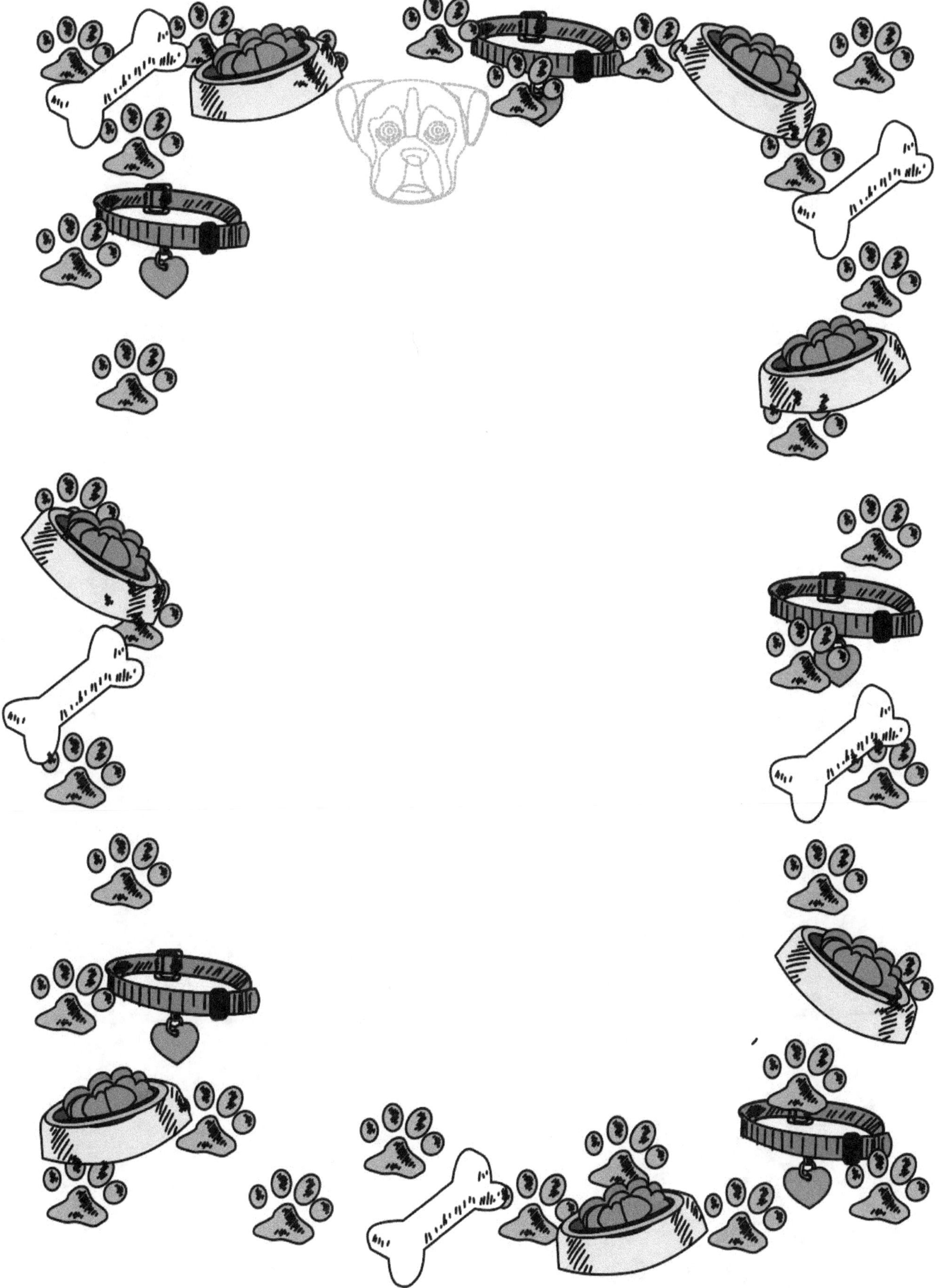

Jack Russell

1

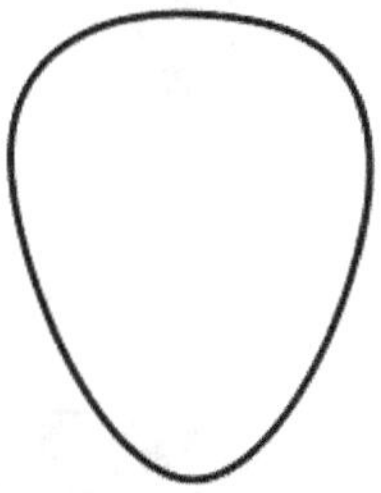

2

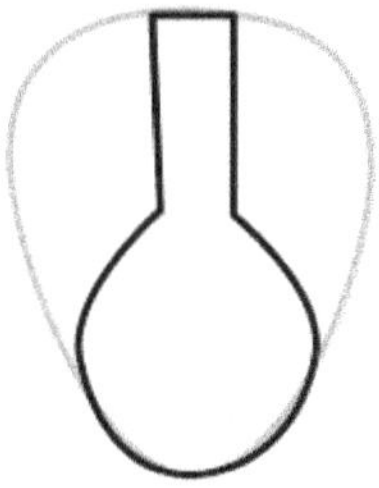

3

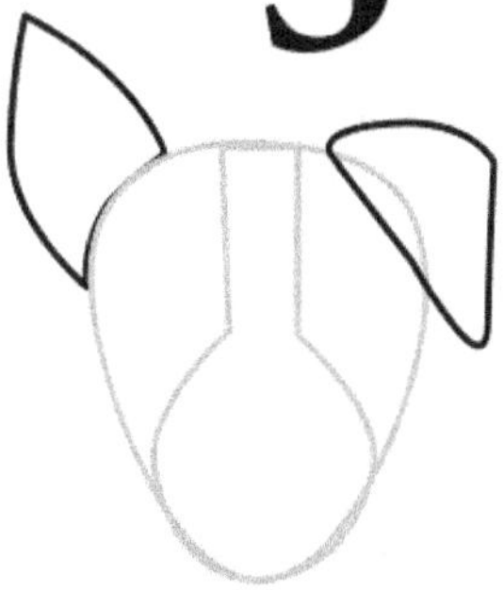

4

5

6

7

8

9

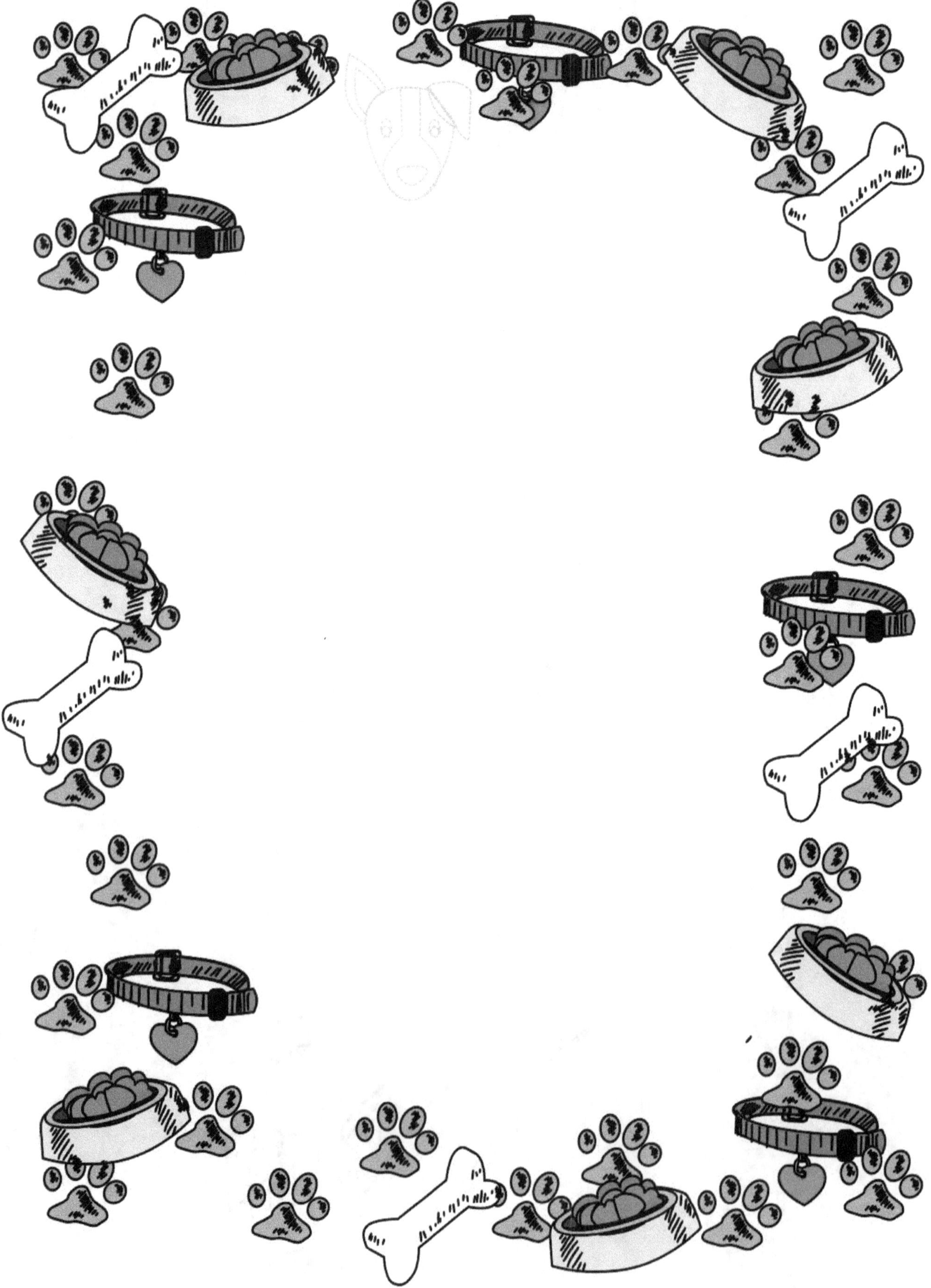

St. Bernard

1

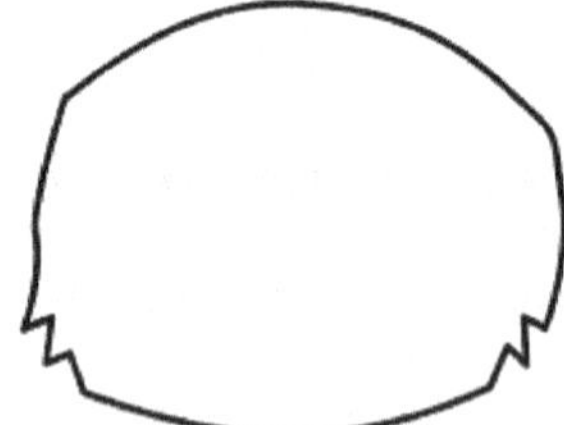

2

3

4

5

6

7

8

9

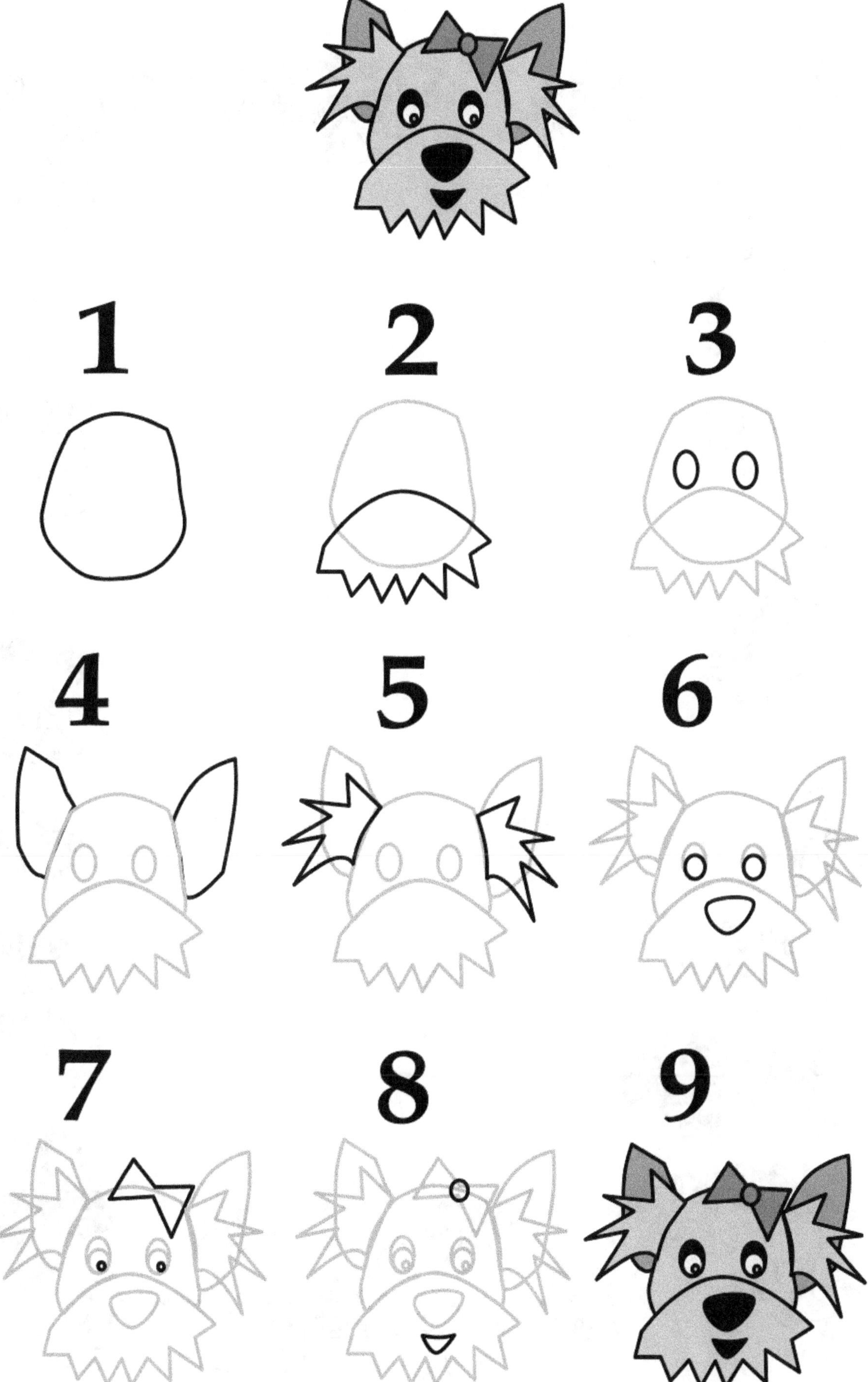

1
2
3
4
5
6
7
8
9

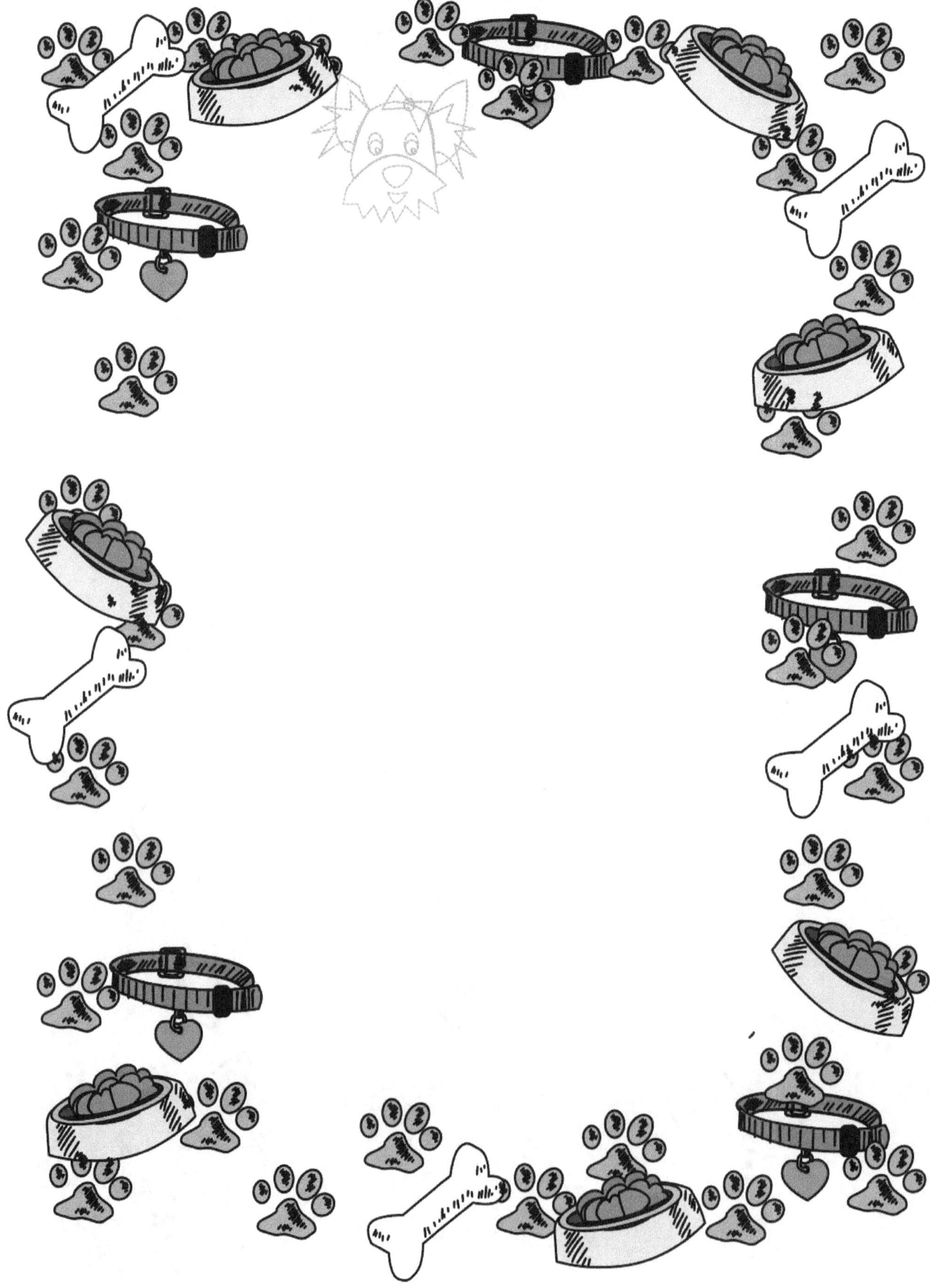

Chihuahua

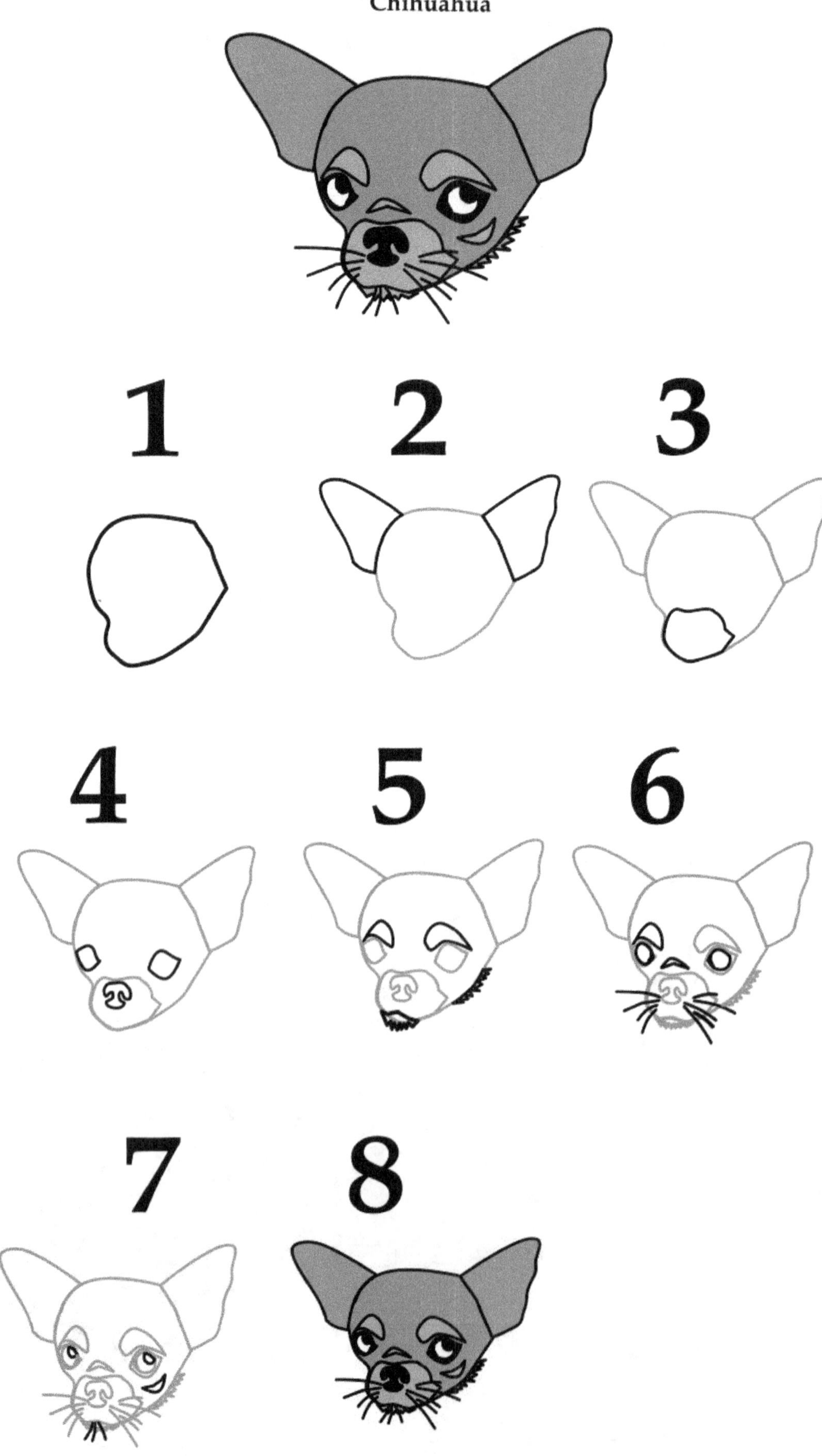

Schnauzer

1   2   3

4   5   6

7   8   9

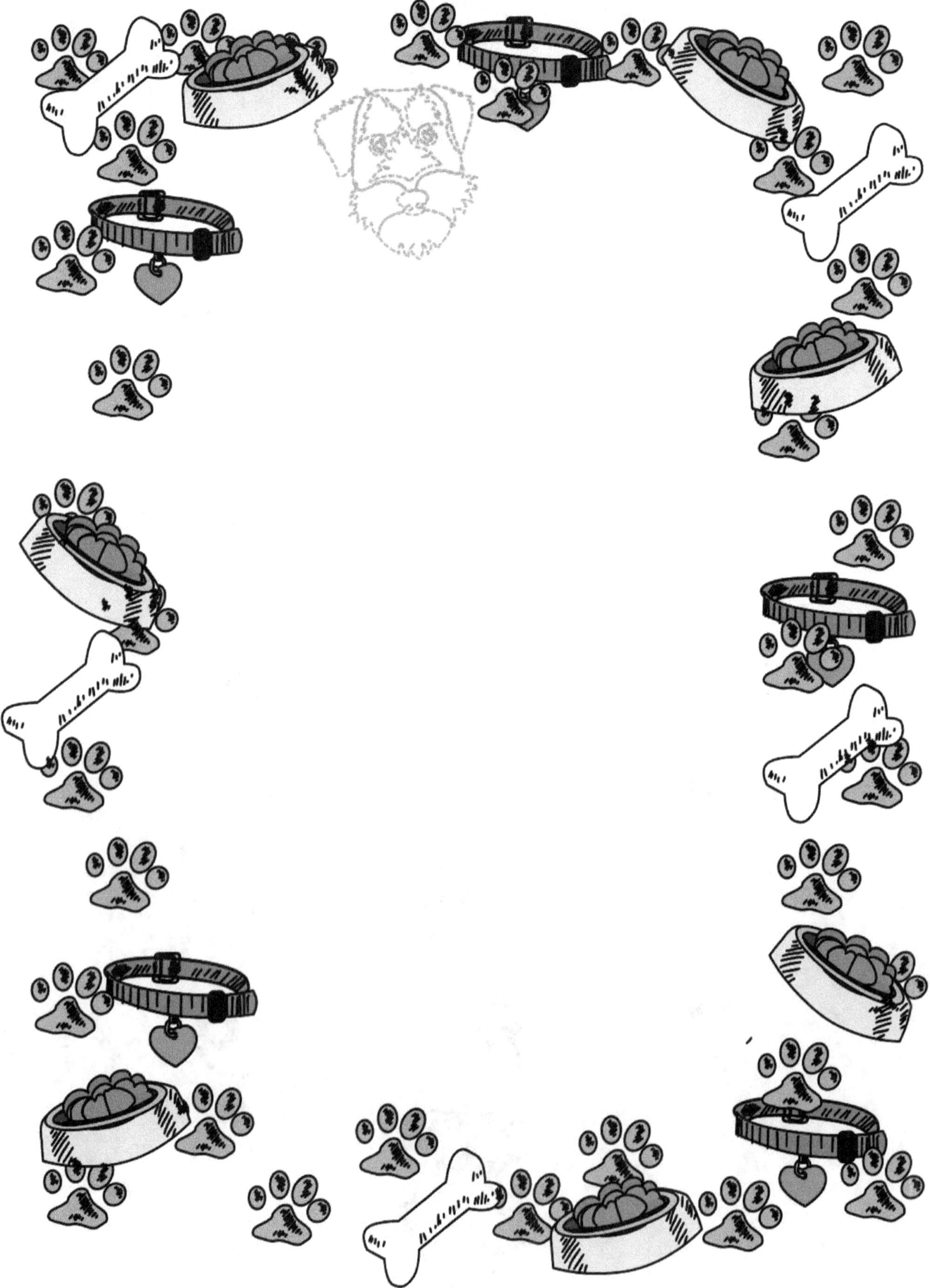

1
2
3
4
5
6
7
8
9

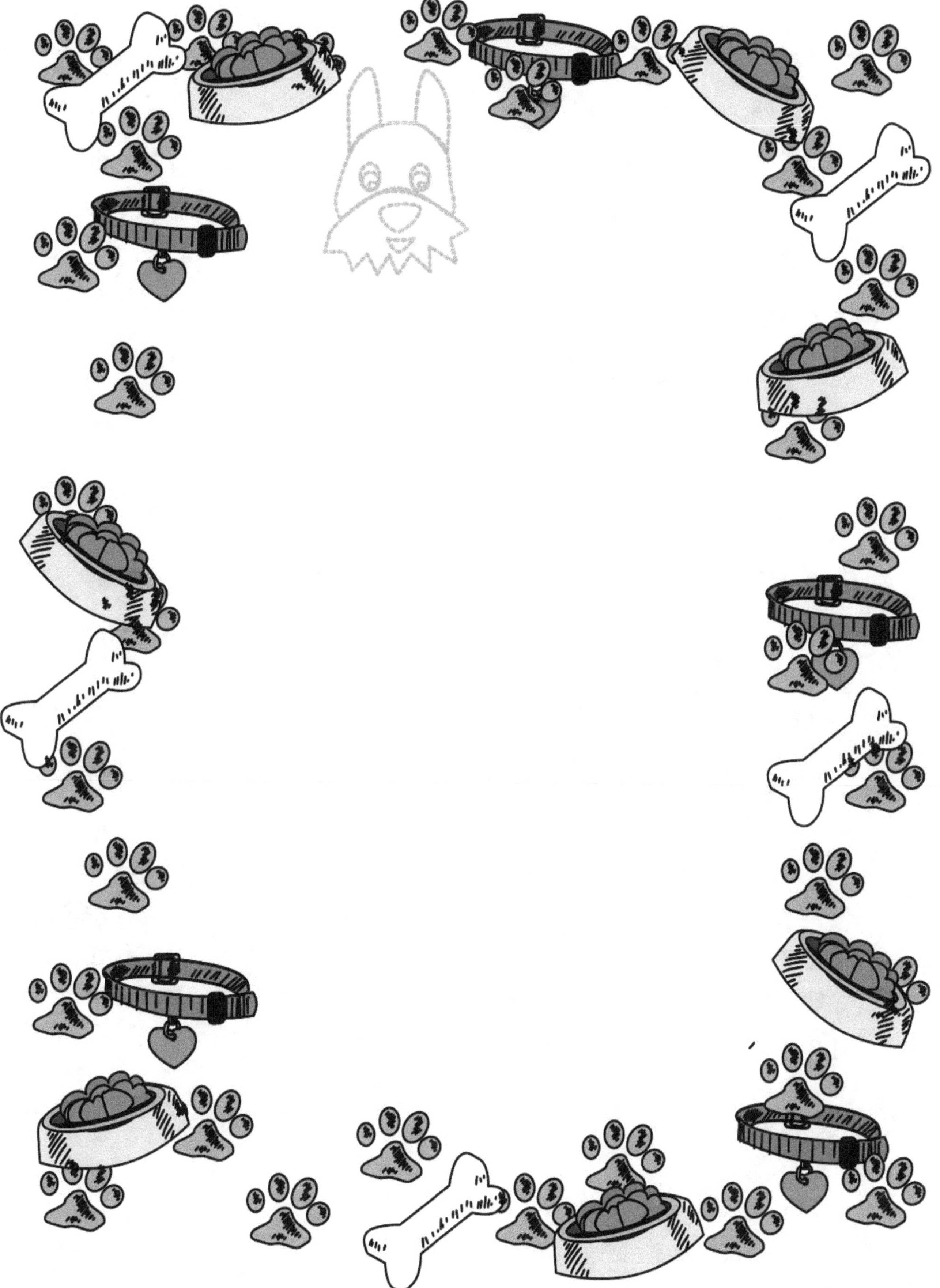

Great Dane

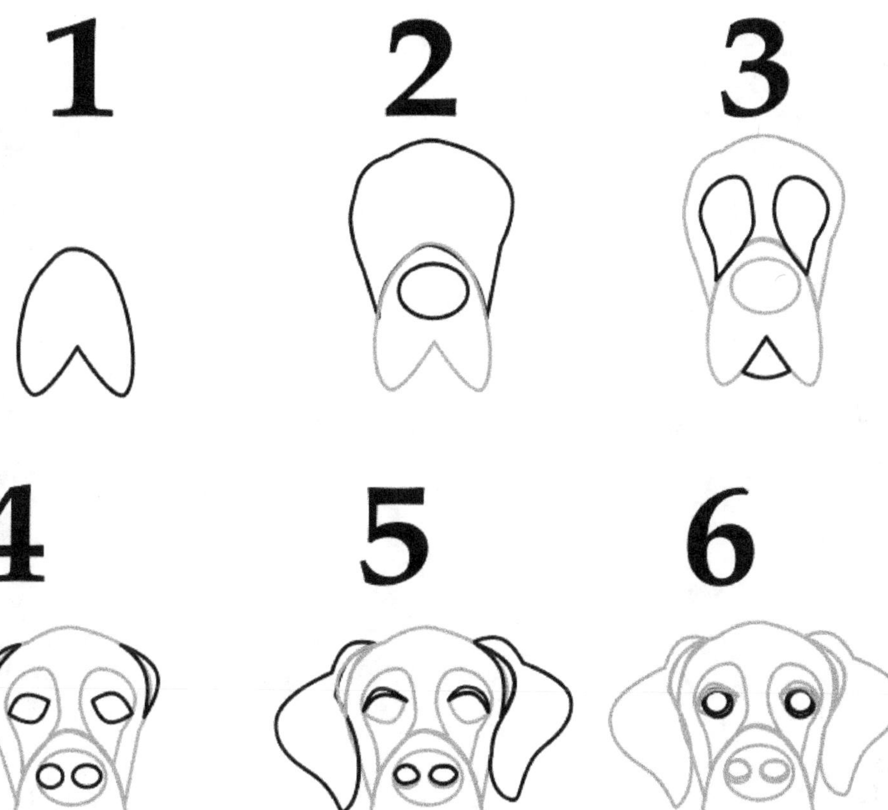

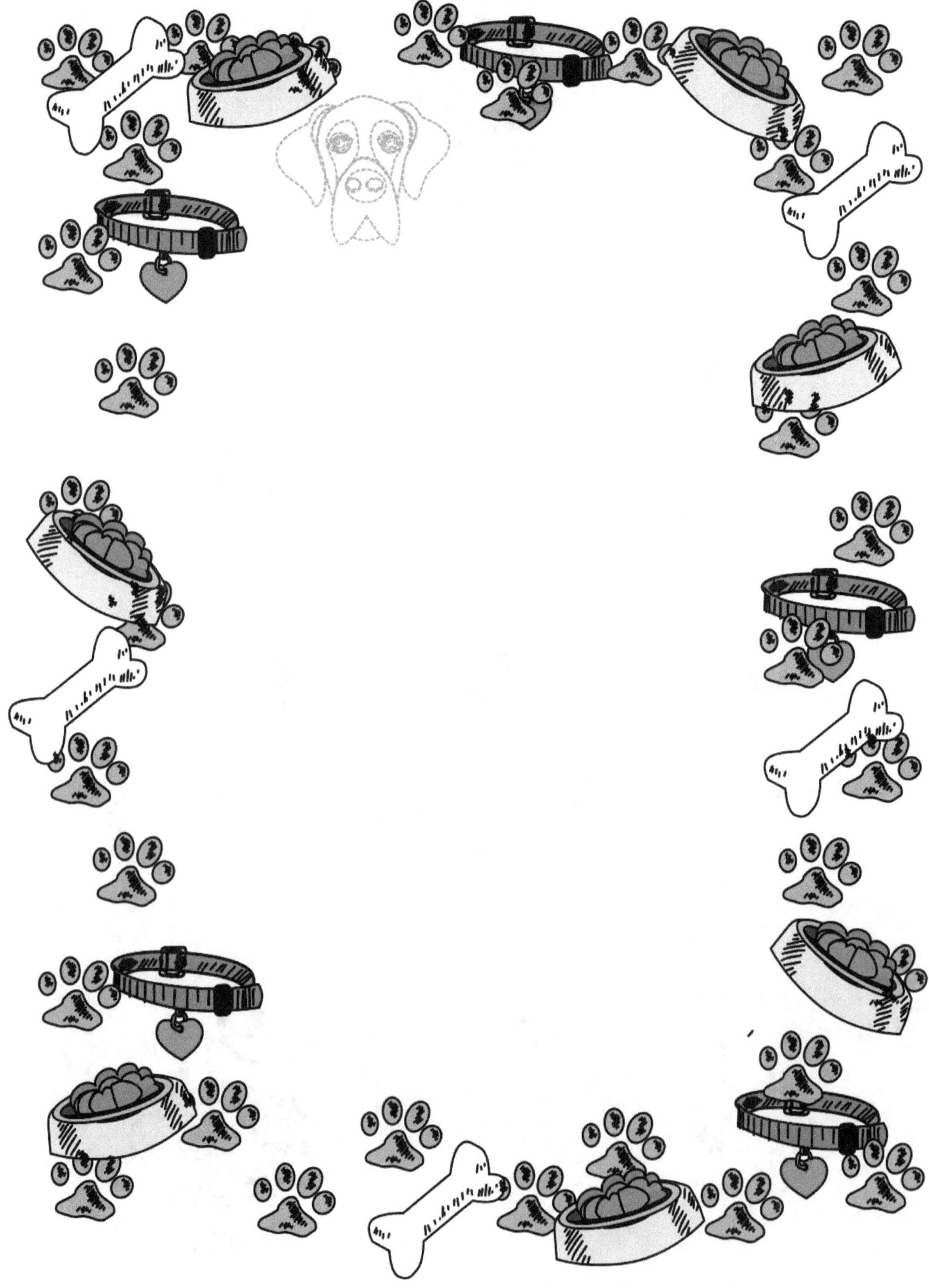

German shepherd

1

2

3

4

5

6

7

8

9

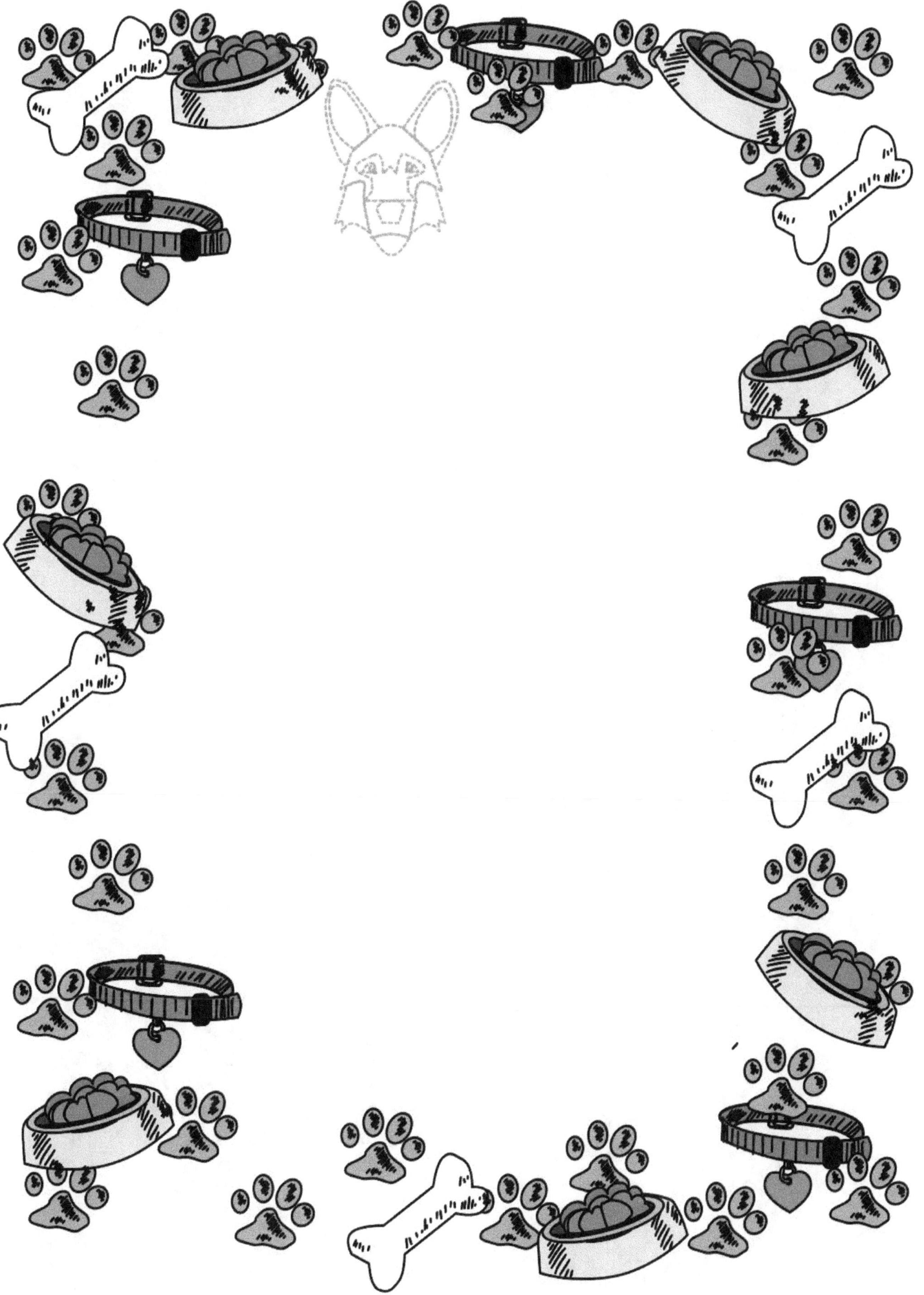

Bulldog

1

2

3

4

5

6

7

8

9

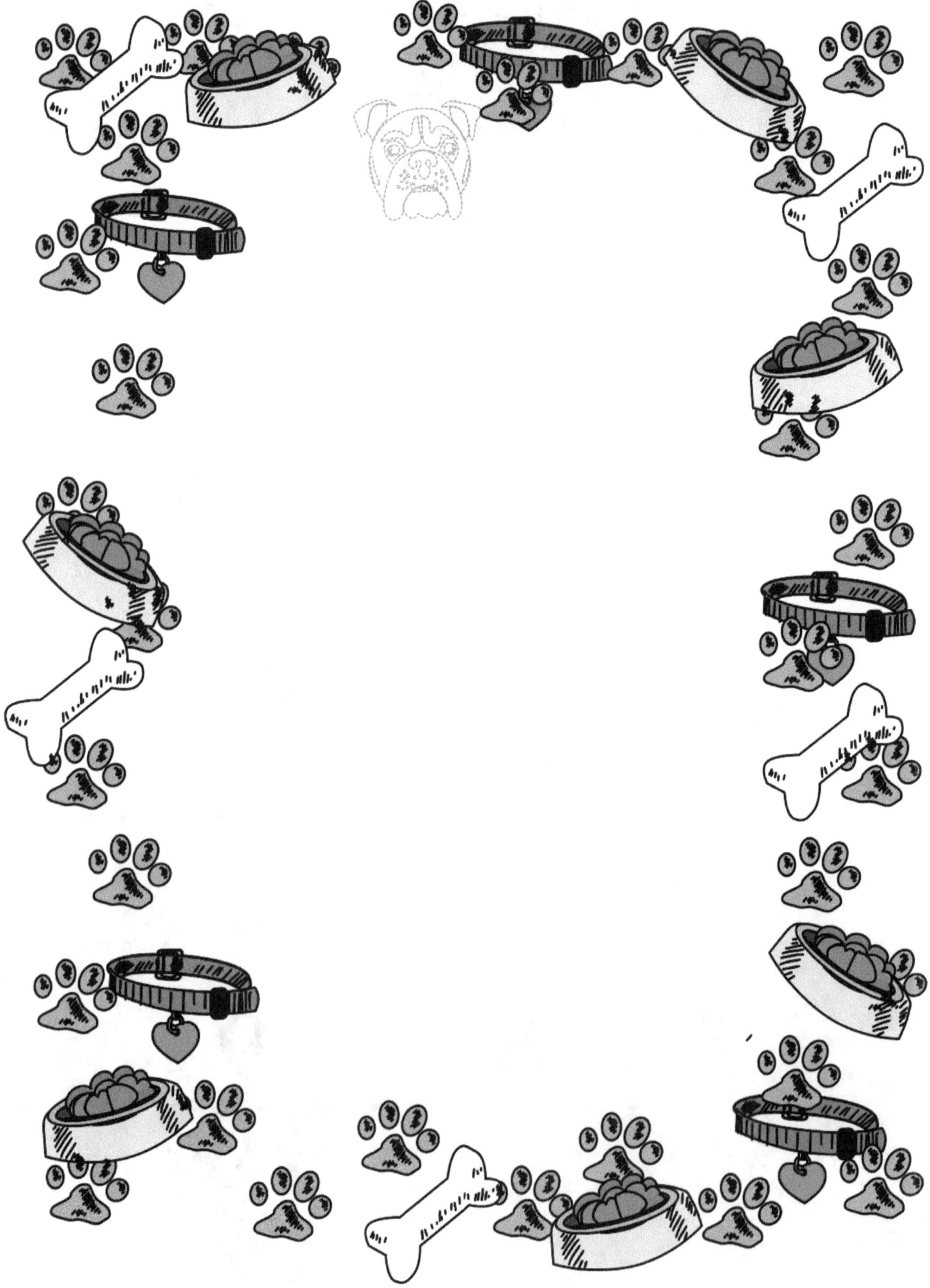

Golden Retriever

1

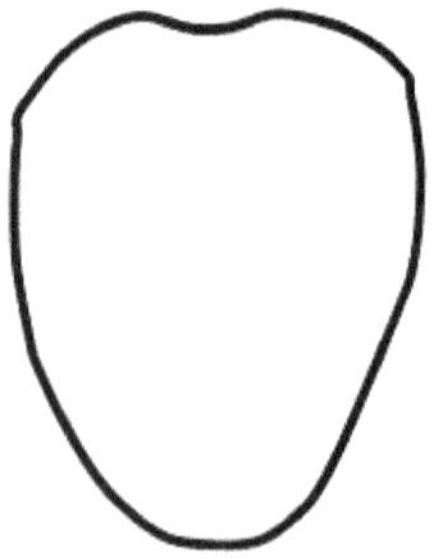

2

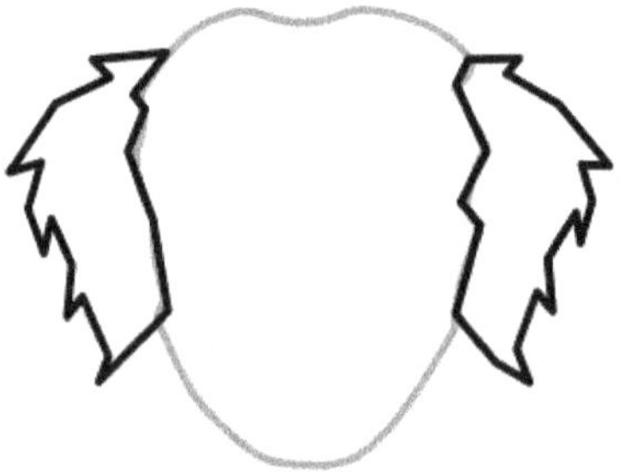

3

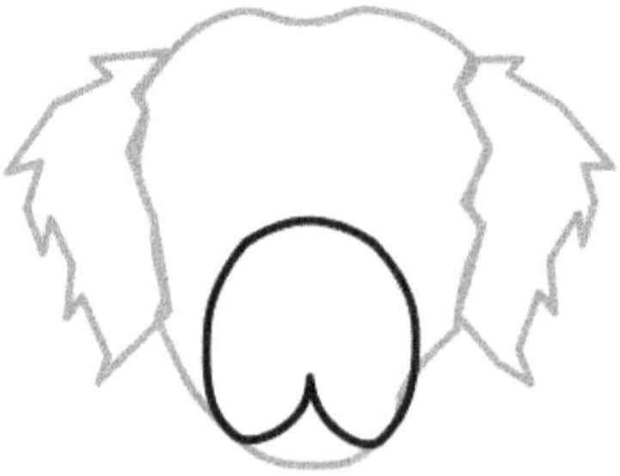

4

5

6

7

8

9

English Bulldog

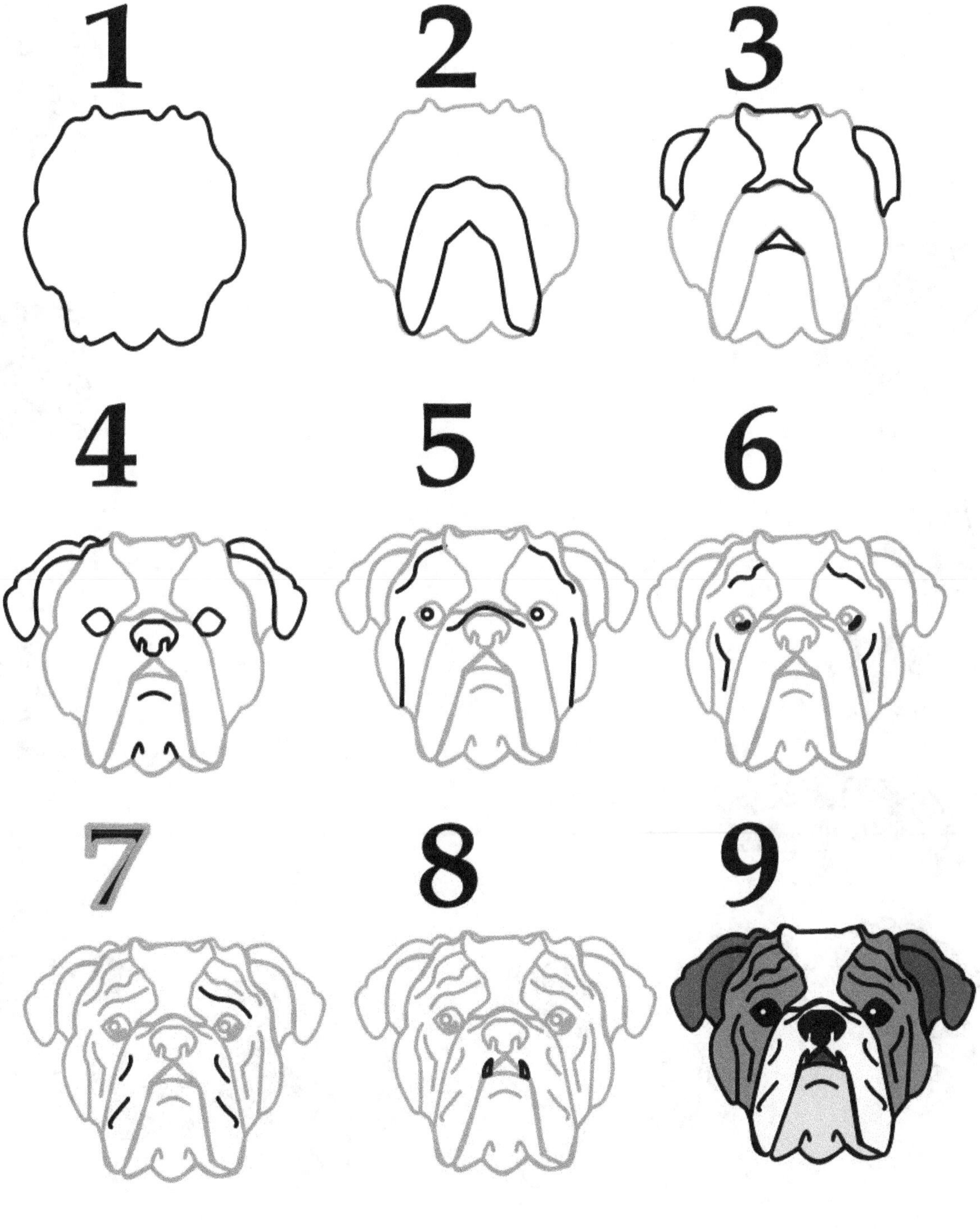

1   2   3

4   5   6

7   8   9

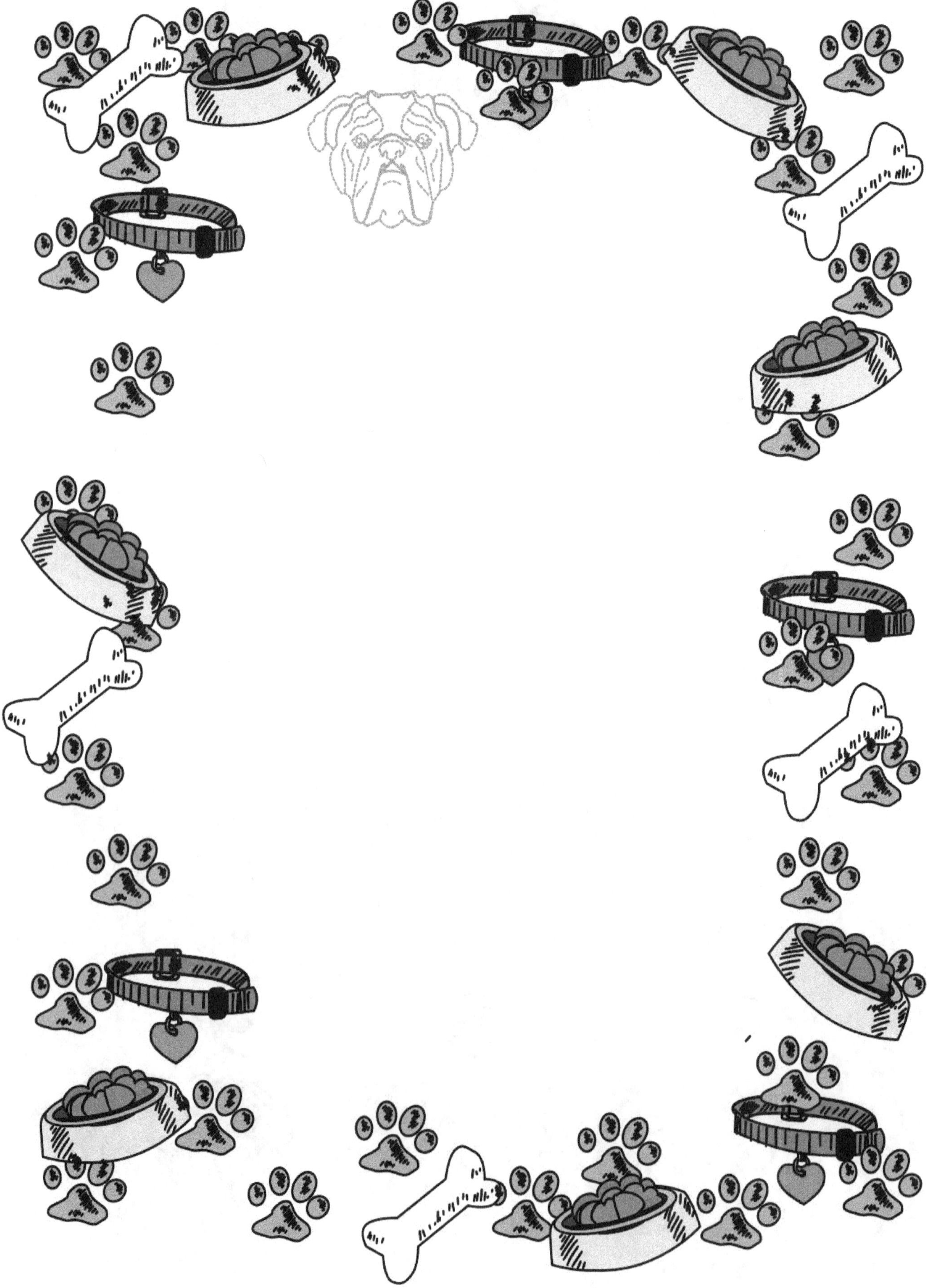

Poodle

1

 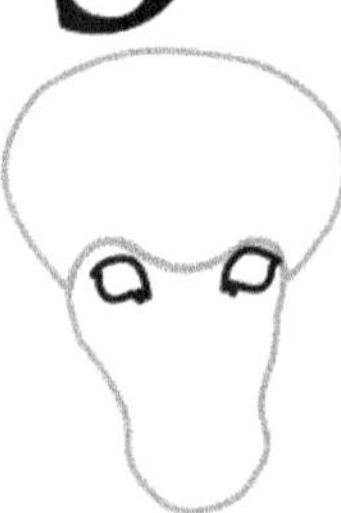

2   3

4   5   6

 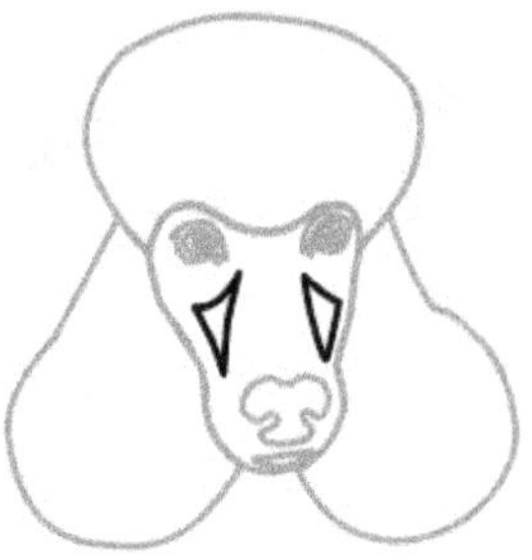 

7   8   9

Dalmatian

1

2

3

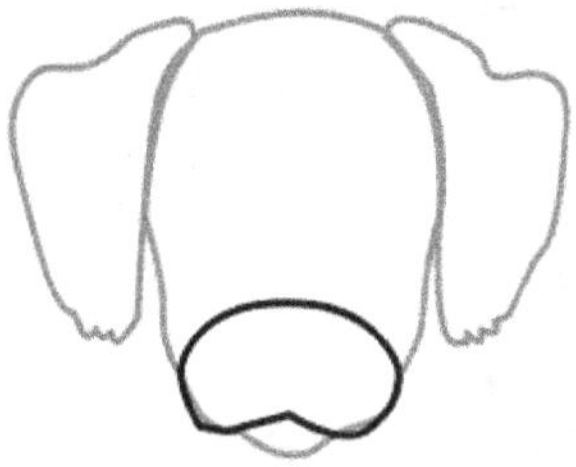

4

5

6

7

8

9

Dachshund

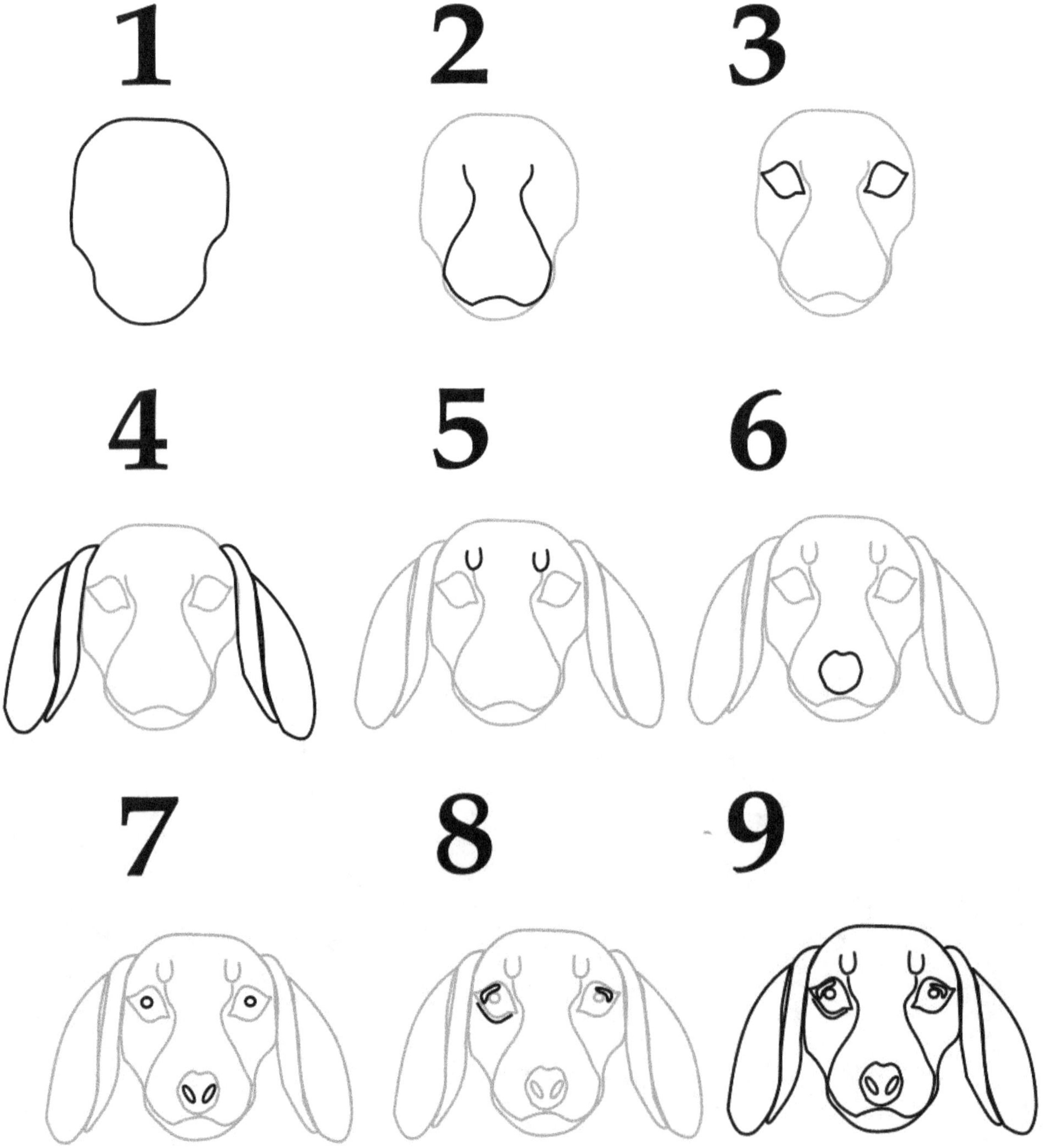

1

2

3

4

5

6

7

8

9

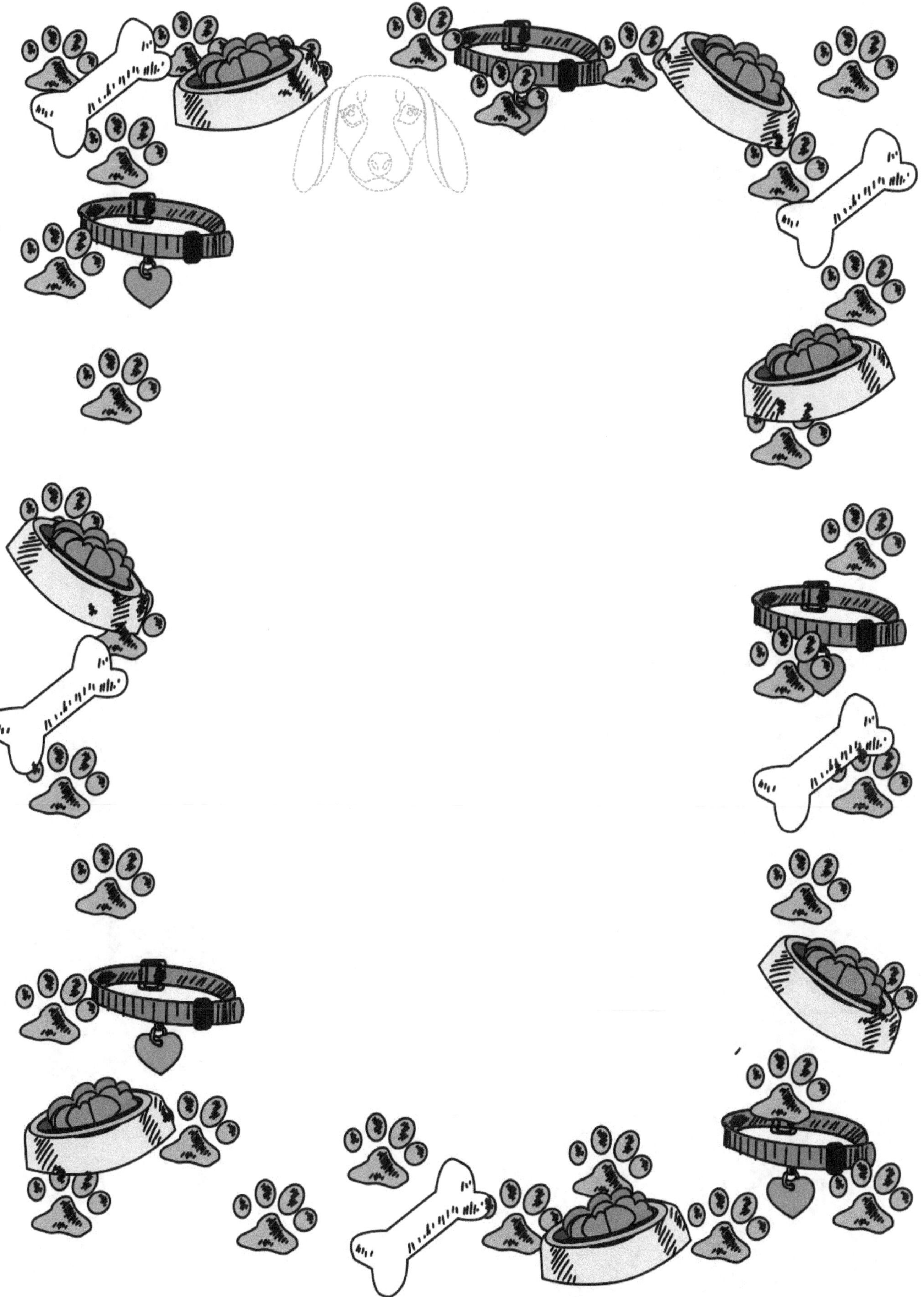

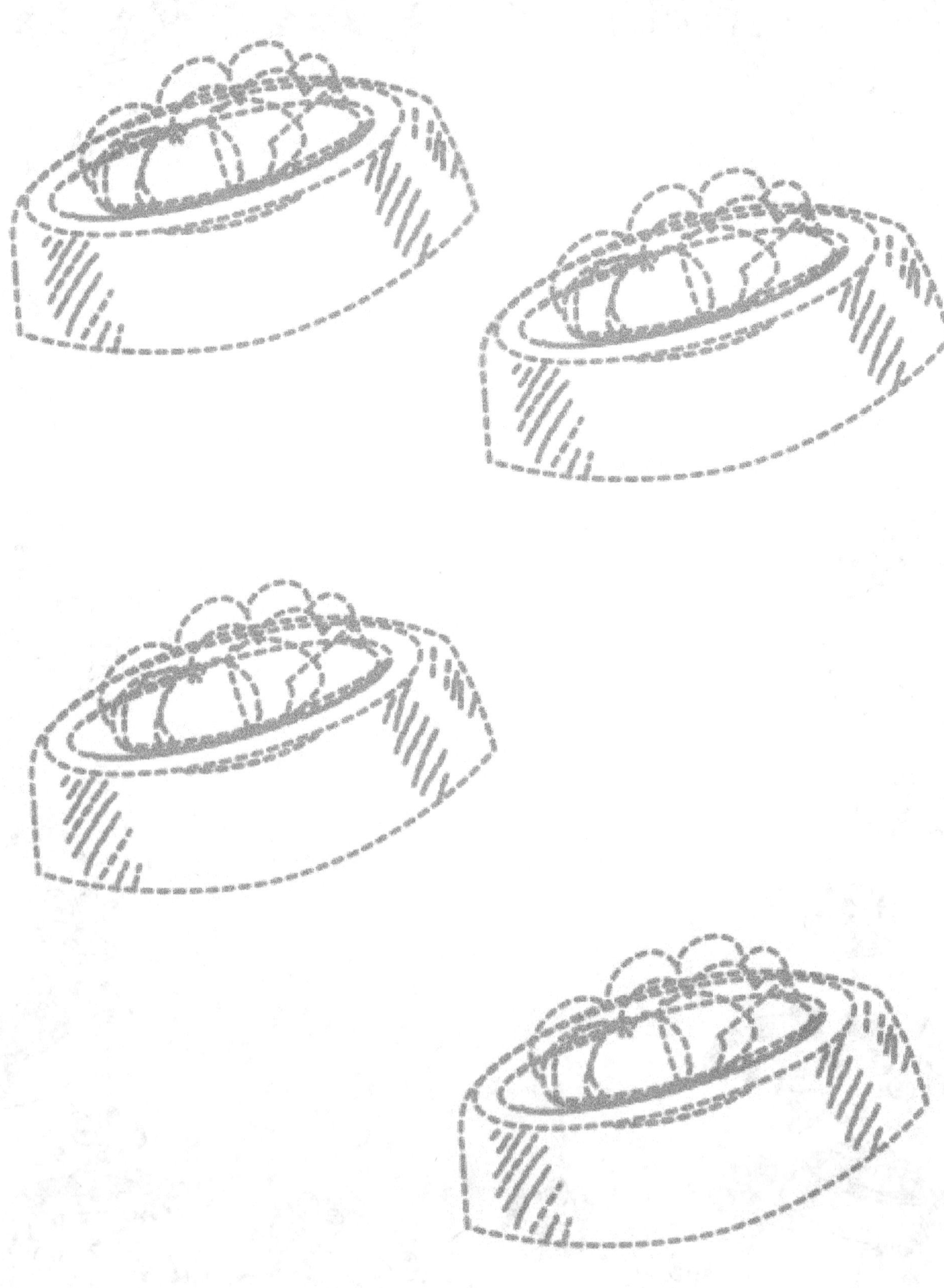

Dog food

1

2

3

4

5

6

7

8

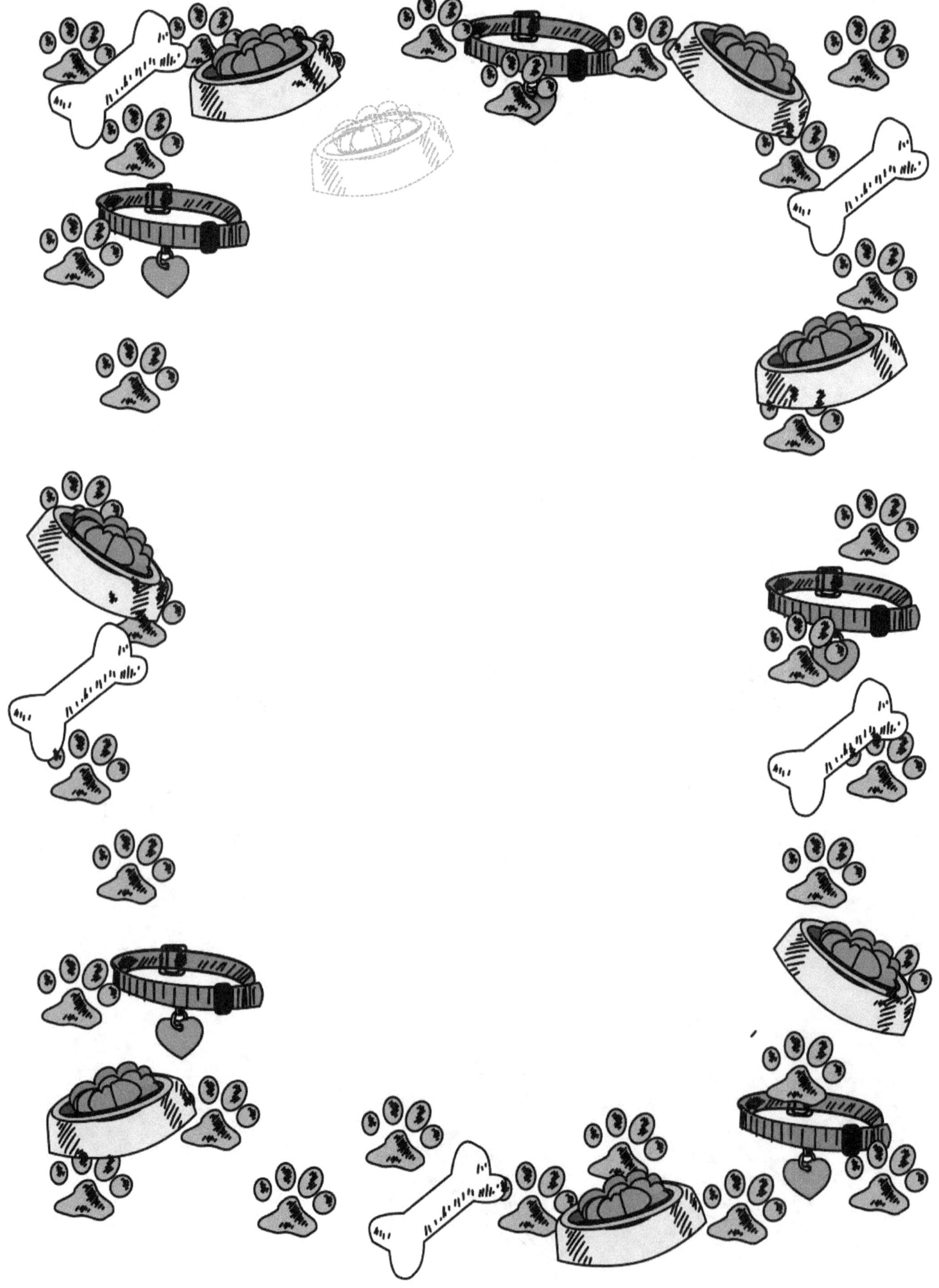

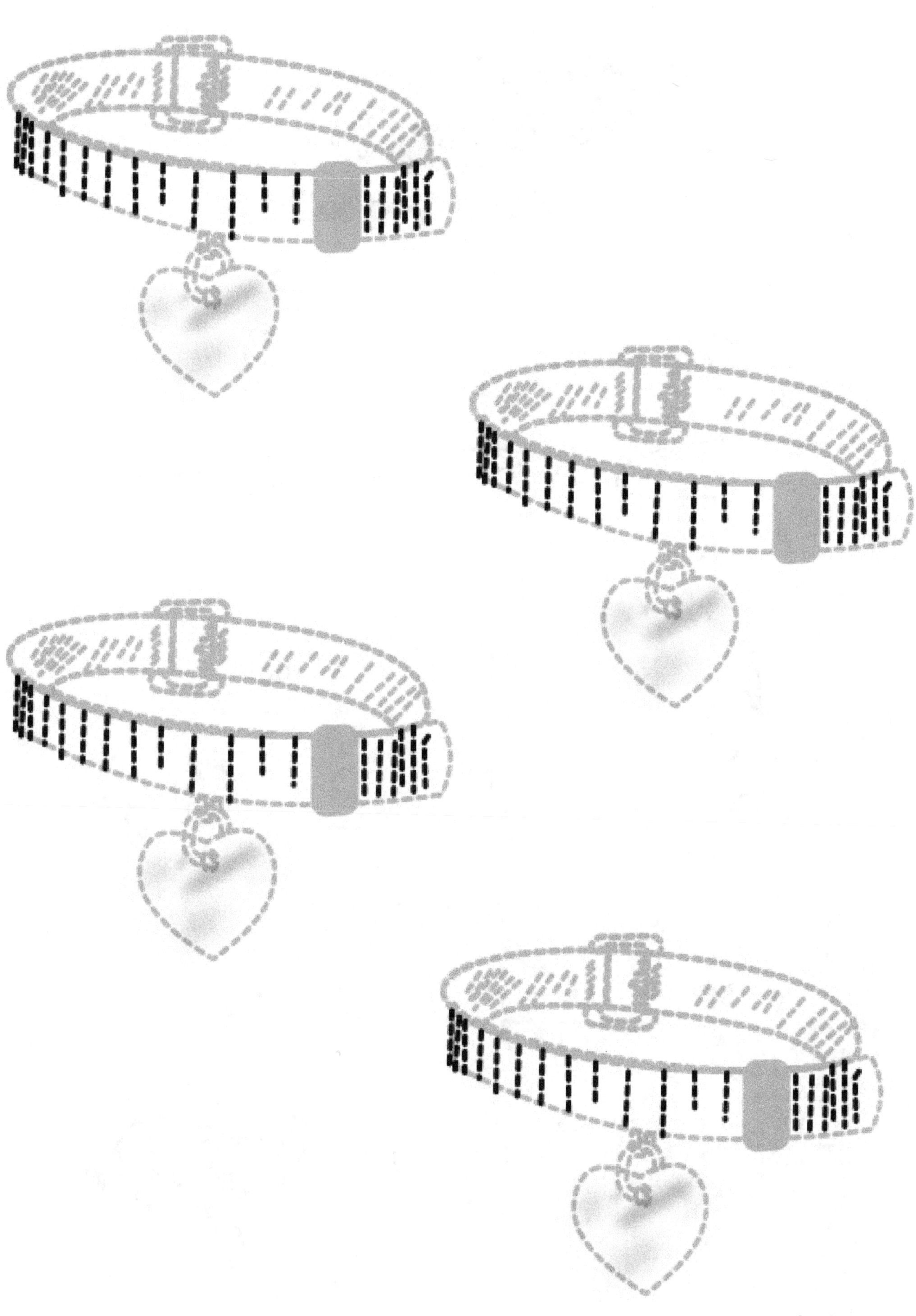

1

2

3

4

5

6

7

8

9

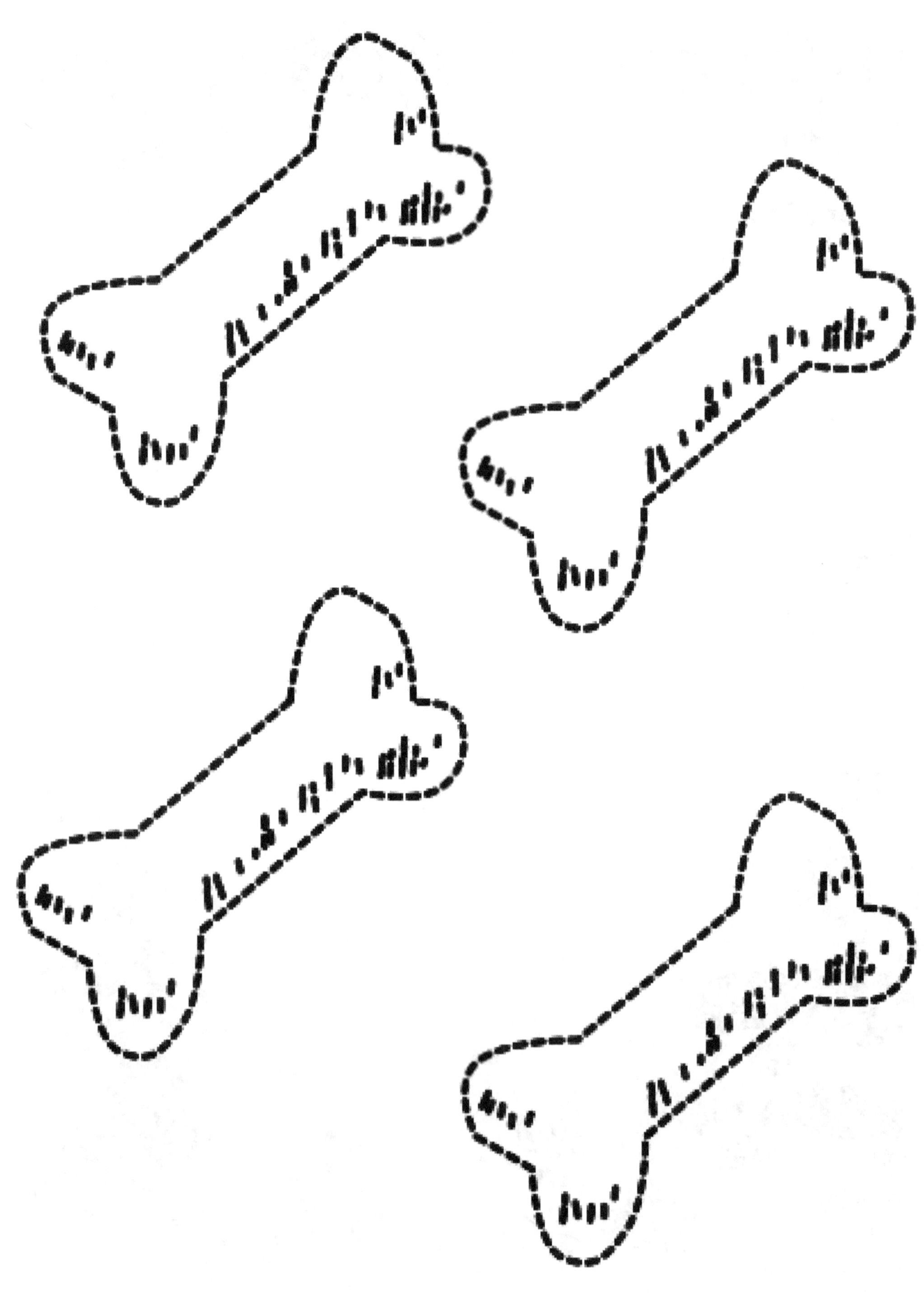

Dog bone

1

2

3

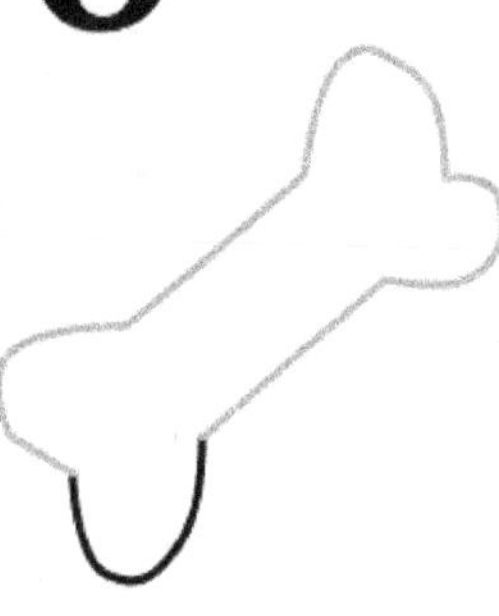

4

5

6

7

8

9

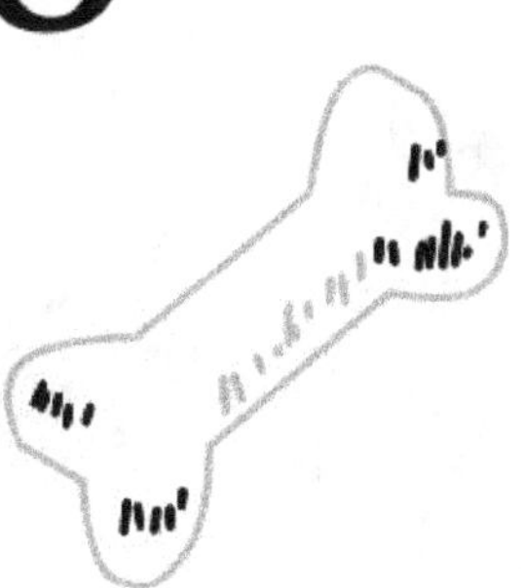

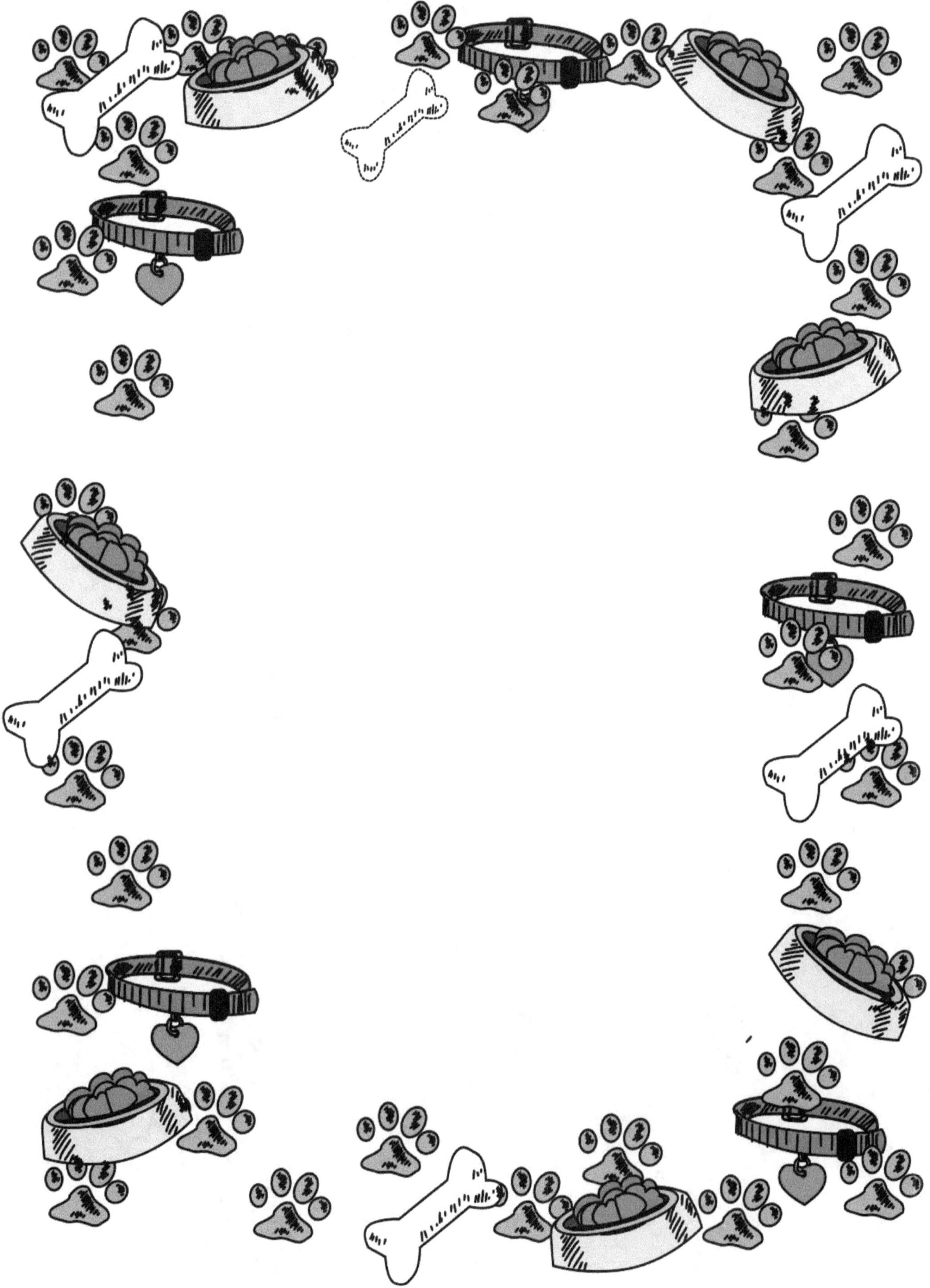

www.ingramcontent.com/pod-product-compliance
Lightning Source LLC
Chambersburg PA
CBHW080003180726
48002CB00020B/2939